50 JAMMIEST BIBLE STORIES

Andy Robb

CWR

Editing, design and production by CWR
Cover image: Andy Robb
Printed in Croatia by Zrinski

ISBN: 978-1-85345-851-4

INTRO

There are some things that are really difficult to do, such as eating jelly with a pair of chopsticks, not slurping through the straw when you get to the bottom of a milkshake and keeping a straight face when someone accidentally burps in the middle of quiet reading at school. But for most people, reading the Bible tops the lot of them.

If you've never so much as taken a sneaky peek between the covers of a Bible (and even if you have), it's sometimes really head-scratchingly tricky to know where exactly to begin. For starters, the Bible isn't one big book, it's lots of smaller books (sixty-six actually) that are all crammed together like a mini-library. The books have all got fancy names, such as Genesis (which is right at the very beginning), Job (pronounced JOBE), Psalms (pronounced SARMS), Mark (which you'll be relieved to know is actually pronounced MARK), Habakkuk (which should get you a pretty good score in a game of Scrabble) and Revelation (which is right at the very end).

Just to make it even more complicated, some of the books have got more than one section (like a sort of Part One and Part Two), and each Bible book doesn't just have chapters like normal books do, they have verses as well (like you get in poems).

So, if you wanted to have a read of chapter twenty and verse seven of the second book of Kings (cos there are two of them), you may find it written like this ...

2 Kings 20:7

... which, to me, looks more like a maths equation than anything to do with the Bible – but that's the way it is.

If you're itching to know what that Bible reference I just used is all about and also to find out how some perfectly good figs were (in my opinion) wasted, then you're going to need to get your hands on a copy of a Bible to check it out. In fact, you'll need a Bible to get the most out of this book, so beg, borrow or buy yourself one as soon as you can.

As it's not always easy to decide which bit of the Bible to read first and in what order you should read it, we've gone and done all the hard work for you. Aren't we kind? In this book are fifty hand-picked Bible stories which are retold in a zappy style and with a colourful cartoon to stop you getting bored. At the end of each story you'll get the chance to find out what happens next (we don't tell you, you've got to do that for yourself – aren't we spoilsports?), and that's when you get to use your Bible. Using the info that we give you about where to find the story in the Bible, you'll need to look it up and then see how the story finishes.

That's about it.

Happy reading and off you go!

EXIT ENOCH

When it comes to living a long life, if you have the good fortune to make it to 100 years old then most people think that you've done really well.

Live to 120 and most of us can't get our heads around it. Well, prepare to have your minds well and truly boggled when I tell you that way back at the beginning of time, the Bible says that people lived heaps longer. We're not talking about 130, 140 or even 150 years old – we're talking centuries!

In Bible book Genesis, chapter 5 there's a check list of some of the world's first people. Kicking off with a guy called Adam (you might have heard of him) right through to a chap called Noah (who is equally famous), it quite helpfully tells you how long each of them lived, and it'll probably blow your mind when I tell you that Adam lived until the ripe old age of 930. Yep, you heard me, 930! That's just 70 years short of a millennium. Wow! OK, so Adam did set a bit of a tough one to beat but his son Seth gave it his best shot and achieved a respectable 912, Adam's grandson Enosh made it to 905 and his great grandson Kenan pipped his dad to the post with 910.

Skipping down the list a bit you come to a chap called Enoch (pronounced EE-NOCK).

For your information Enoch was the great, great, great,

great grandson of Adam and, although he didn't live as long as everyone else, he had a rather unusual claim to fame.

Everyone else, when they came to the end of their lives, died like normal people do. But Enoch wasn't like everyone else. The Bible says that he had a pretty special friendship with God all the time he lived on earth and, when he had reached the age of 365, he didn't pop his clogs (die) like the rest of them. He simply went straight to heaven, just like that. God whipped Enoch away to be with Him. How jammy is that? The Bible doesn't say why, but my guess is that God enjoyed Enoch's company so much He couldn't wait any longer to have him up there in heaven alongside Him.

Isn't it amazing that God so passionately loves the people He has made?

Just to let you know, Enoch's son got the record for the world's oldest person, ever.

Find out who he was and how long he lived in Bible book Genesis, chapter 5 and verses 25 to 27.

2
ALTAR AGGRO

This jammy Bible story is all about how God gave a bunch of people (called the Israelites) some land to live on. Canaan was going to be the base from which God would launch Jesus into the world many centuries later.

Unfortunately it wasn't quite as straightforward as perhaps the Israelites might have liked. There were people already living in Canaan, so the first job their leader Joshua had was to turf these baddies out.

After more than their fair share of battles, the Israelites eventually conquered the land (well, most of it).

Phew! They could finally settle down and make themselves at home.

The Israelites were made up of twelve tribes in all, and two and a half of them (Reuben, Gad and East Manasseh) had been promised some land the opposite side of the river Jordan from Canaan once the fighting was over.

Joshua was as good as his word and sent these two and a half tribes off with his blessing.

And that's when the trouble started.

The Israelites worshipped and made sacrifices to God in a big tent called the Tabernacle. It occurred to the leaders of these two and a half tribes that, in years to come, the Israelite tribes who had settled in Canaan might forget that Reuben, Gad and East Manasseh were part of them. Worse than that, they might no longer allow them back across the river to worship God at the tabernacle. So they hit upon a plan. Before leaving Canaan they built a stone altar beside the river Jordan to remind everyone of the fact that they were all one big happy Israelite family.

Did the tribes in Canaan see it like that? Nope. The rest of the Israelites thought the altar had been set up in competition with the tabernacle and they were all for having a civil war over it.

A delegation of tribal leaders headed up by a fellow called Phinehas went to find out what was going on just in case there had been some sort of misunderstanding.

Did Phinehas and his entourage believe their story or were the tribes of Reuben, Gad and East Manasseh wiped out in war by their own people?

YOU'VE GOTTA 'ALTAR' YOUR BEHAVIOUR

All is revealed in Bible book Joshua, chapter 22 and verses 30 to 34.

AXE-IDENT!

If you want to talk to someone you've got plenty of options. Face to face, by phone, by email, by text, or any number of other ways. When God wanted to speak to people (particularly in the Old Testament part of the Bible), He would do it through people called prophets. They were hand-picked by God to tune in to what He was saying and then to pass the message on.

One such prophet was Elisha.

He'd taken over from a chap called Elijah (yes, I know it's a bit confusing having such similar names but there's not much I can do about it now) and was pretty well known round and about for having performed many amazing miracles in God's power, one of which was bringing a young man back to life.

Elisha was a bit of a celebrity in the world of prophets and was the leader of a school of prophets who all looked up to the great man.

Although he might have been a bit of a big-shot prophet, when it came to doing miracles no miracle was too small for Elisha.

One of Elisha's pupils had suggested that they think about building a bigger meeting place. Elisha was up for it so off they all went to chop down some wood to make the building.

The location they'd picked was by the River Jordan, but that was their downfall.

Just when things were in full swing there was a splash and a gasp as one of the prophets discovered to his horror that his axe-head had fallen off into the water.

A fuss about nothing you might say, but the poor fellow's axe was not his own. He'd borrowed it. And, if you know anything about axe-heads you'll know that floating is not something they do very well.

What was the prophet to do?

Fear not! Elisha the miracle-working prophet to the rescue!

Want to find out how Elisha saved the day?

Read the jammy ending in Bible book 2 Kings, chapter 6 and verses 6 to 7.

4
PROPHET POWER

The Bible has a few stories in it about dead people coming back to life. Probably the most well-known is when Jesus (God's Son) was raised from the dead by God after spending three days in a tomb. And it's Jesus as well who takes the credit for bringing back to life a guy called Lazarus after being dead for four days, the daughter of a guy called Jairus and a young man who was on his way to the cemetery.

The rather jammy Bible story I am about to recount didn't actually involve Jesus but it did have everything to do with God's power.

Here's what happened.

Elisha (an awesome prophet of God) was poorly and was on his death bed. Jehoash, the king of Israel was inconsolable and didn't want him to die.

Elisha was Israel's secret weapon and with the powerful prophet on their side they had an advantage over their enemies. What would they do without him? Well, he was about to find out because, for all King Jehoash's blubbing, he could do nothing and Elisha died.

Elisha was buried in a tomb and that, you would think, would be the end of his power to do miracles.

Not so!

Israel's Moabite enemy had sent raiding parties into the land to cause trouble.

The Bible tells us that at the very same time some Israelites were busy burying a man's body. Bad timing!

On spotting the Moabite raiders, the Israelites panicked, flung the man's body into Elisha's tomb and then scarpered. Bet they'd have been surprised to see what happened next!

BULLSEYE!

Elisha's Tomb

Head for Bible book 2 Kings, chapter 13 and verse 21 for something really jammy.

5
NIGHT FLIGHT

If you know the Christmas story about Jesus' birth then you won't need to be told about the wise men who dropped in on Jesus to worship Him.

What a lot of people don't know is what happened after that.

When these wise men (visitors from a distant land) showed up in Jerusalem to get directions from King Herod of how to find this new born King, they didn't realise that the king was not as pleased to see them as he made out. Although Herod pretended that he was also interested in popping in to pay his respects to Jesus, he actually had absolutely no intention of doing anything of the sort. As far as he was concerned there was only room for one ruler in Israel, and he was it. King Herod was not a happy bunny and the only reason he wanted to discover the whereabouts of Jesus was to kill Him. The sooner this young upstart was out of the way the better.

Anyway, once these wise men had found Jesus and had presented Him with gifts of gold, frankincense and myrrh, they were warned by God (in a dream) not to let on to Herod where Jesus was and to go back home by another route.

When Herod found out that these visitors had double-crossed him he was hopping mad.

The cruel tyrant gave the order for his men to kill every boy of two years old or younger, who lived in or near Bethlehem. That way he reckoned he would be sure to snuff out the life of Jesus once and for all.

What Herod hadn't counted on was God giving Joseph, (Jesus' dad) the heads-up that the conniving king was on the warpath. In a dream Joseph was instructed to escape with his wife (Mary) and Jesus to the land of Egypt and to wait there until King Herod had died.

Jesus might have had a jammy escape but Herod knew none of this and still went ahead with his dastardly plan.

Want to know how Joseph knew when it was safe to return?

Find out in Bible book Matthew, chapter 2 and verses 19 to 23.

THAT'S YER LOT

When Jesus was on the earth He had a tip-top team of twelve disciples to help Him do His stuff.

It was one of these twelve close friends who cheated on Jesus and betrayed Him to the religious leaders so that they could put Jesus on trial and have Him killed.

Jesus always knew that Judas would double-cross Him, but that was part of God's plan.

Judas bitterly regretted what he'd done and the Bible has two accounts of how he met his end.

One story has it that Judas hanged himself and the other that he fell headlong into a field (that he'd bought with the 30 pieces of silver he got for betraying his Master) and his intestines spilled out. Yuck!

Mix the two together and it could have been that Judas hanged himself and when the corpse fell to the ground his body burst open. You choose.

Either way, the point is that Judas was a 'goner' and, with Jesus now back in heaven, the disciples had work to do. Minus Judas though, they were now a man down.

The disciples figured that if Jesus thought it was important for there to be twelve in the team then there was nothing for it. A replacement had to be found.

Whoever it was, needed to have hung out with Jesus right from the word go, to have been at Jesus' crucifixion and then to have seen Jesus when He'd been raised from the dead.

That sort of narrowed the field a bit and the Bible tells us that it came down to a run-off between a couple of guys. Joseph called Barsabbas, also known as Justus (yes, I know that's a bit confusing), and Matthias who, fortunately for us, only had the one name.

So who was God's choice to replace Judas?

Well, the way the Jewish people often used to decide God's will was by casting lots, which looked a bit like dice but had words (the answers) instead of dots. This wasn't gambling. They believed that God would make sure the end result was what He wanted.

Which of them got a jammy promotion into this elite group?

A BIG LET-DOWN

When it came to big-time Bible baddies, as far as Christians in the world's first church (in Jerusalem) were concerned, it was no contest. Saul of Tarsus won hands down. He was the man they all feared. Saul was a Jew who was hell-bent on wiping Christians off the face of the earth and, if he hadn't been stopped in his tracks by Jesus, who knows what would have happened!

After a life-changing encounter with Jesus, Saul immediately changed his ways and became Jesus' biggest fan. What a turnaround! Saul had been on his way to the city of Damascus to get his hands on as many Christians as he could and have them thrown into jail. Now Saul was keen as mustard to tell as many people as possible about Jesus.

To do this Saul headed off to the Jewish synagogues to fill his fellow Jews in on his amazing experience of Jesus.

To be honest, they were a wee bit baffled by Saul. One minute he was Number One Enemy of the Christians and now you couldn't shut him up about how great being a Christian was (not that they were called Christians quite yet).

While the Jewish religious leaders tried to work out what was going on, Saul simply went from strength to strength. Soon the penny dropped that a man with Saul's passion and

intelligence could make life really difficult for them. The last thing the religious leaders needed were heaps of Jews becoming followers of Jesus. They thought they'd seen the last of Jesus when He'd been crucified on a cross in Jerusalem a while back and now it looked like His name was on everyone's lips again.

Saul had to be stopped, and quickly.

A plan was hatched to kill Saul, but Saul soon got wind of it.

Day and night, the Jews who were against him kept their eagle eyes on the city gates so that he couldn't escape.

Who won the day? Did Saul have a jammy escape?

Check out Bible book Acts, chapter 9 and verse 25 to find out.

A SPIT SPAT

When Jesus lived on earth He loved demonstrating how much God cared for people by healing them. This Bible story is all about that.

Jesus and His disciples were out and about when they came across a beggar who had been blind from birth.

While the disciples had a good old ponder as to why he'd been born this way (had his parents done something wrong? Had he done something wrong?) Jesus got stuck in. As far as Jesus was concerned, if this man got healed by God's power then all those questions didn't matter. All that mattered was that God got the credit.

Anyone who'd hung around Jesus for a while would soon have discovered that Jesus healed people in loads of different ways. There was no one formula that He worked to. And this particular day was no exception.

I suppose that Jesus could have just placed His hands on the man's eyes and healed him, but He didn't. Instead He spat on the ground, made some mud with the saliva, and then put it on the man's eyes. Having done this, Jesus told the man to go and wash in the Pool of Siloam.

And, guess what! The blind man was healed.

Was the blind man just jammy that Jesus happened to have

been passing by, or did God plan it all along? Who knows? One thing's for sure, his healing started a right old rumpus.

Some Jewish religious leaders heard that the chap had got his sight back and interrogated him to find out how exactly it had happened.

The thing that bugged them most seemed to be that Jesus had healed the blind man on the Jewish Sabbath. It didn't seem to make a blind bit of difference (pardon the pun) that the guy could now see. You'd think they'd be over the moon but they weren't. According to their traditions you weren't supposed to do any work (and that included healing!) on the Sabbath. If you did, it meant you were breaking the law.

So, because in their eyes Jesus had broken Jewish law, He was a sinner and they were none too pleased.

YOU DON'T BELIEVE ME. I CAN SEE THAT!

Head for Bible book John, chapter 9 and verse 16 to discover precisely what they thought of Jesus.

9

SATURDAY NIGHT FEVER

We catch up with Jesus in this jammy Bible story not long after He'd begun to let on that He wasn't just an ordinary carpenter from Nazareth (His home town) but God's one and only Son. Jesus didn't need to blab about it. It was obvious by the things He said and did that He was different.

Jesus had recently been baptised in the River Jordan after which a voice from heaven had been heard saying, 'You are my own dear Son, and I am pleased with you.' Then, a little while later, to everyone's astonishment Jesus healed a man in the synagogue in Capernaum. Synagogues were a bit like churches for the Jewish people and every Sabbath (Saturday) Jews met to be taught from their Scriptures. Jesus got invited to do a spot of teaching on this particular day and everyone was amazed at the way He spoke and taught with such authority. It was as if He really understood what the Scriptures meant. That was no surprise. He was God's Son after all.

Jesus was on a mission to get people back to being friends with God and He was gradually pulling together a team of disciples to help Him do it. Some were with Him at the synagogue and, while the congregation scratched their heads trying to puzzle out who this miracle-working Man was, Jesus headed out to the home of a couple of them, Simon and Andrew.

When they got there Jesus was told that Simon's mother-in-law wasn't well. She'd come down with a fever and was bed-bound.

Jesus was having none of that. Sickness wasn't God's idea and Jesus knew it.

The Bible doesn't even say that Jesus prayed for the poorly lady; He simply took Simon's mother-in-law by the hand and the fever left her.

With Simon's mother-in-law back on her feet she was able to rustle up a scrummy meal for the lot of 'em. Bet people thought she was jammy having Jesus drop by!

Did Jesus then have a quiet night in and put His feet up?

Bible book Mark, chapter 1 and verses 32 to 34 will reveal all.

10
PAY DAY

When Jesus wanted to explain something about God He would often tell a story to make His point. These stories were called parables and one of them that Jesus told was about how God made it possible for everyone to go to heaven regardless of whether they accepted His invitation while they were young or when they were old.

Jesus told the story of a landowner who went out early in the morning to hire labourers to work on his vineyard. This guy offered to pay them a denarius (a silver coin) for a day's work. Yep, that sounded good and so they set to it.

A little later in the day (around nine in the morning) the landowner went off to get some more labourers to work in his vineyard. Sure enough he soon found what he was looking for and he set them to work as well.

He did the same at midday, at three in the afternoon and then at five o'clock. The chances are that probably having begun work at around six in the morning the working day would finish around six in the evening. That meant that the last lot would only have to put in an hour's labour. Oh well, never mind. At least they'd get a little bit of money, which was better than nothing.

That's precisely what the labourers who'd been slaving away since the crack of dawn thought. It had been tough working through the heat of the day. Surely they deserved to receive a bigger payout for their endeavours?

'Fraid not chaps! The landowner in the story represented God, and Jesus wanted His listeners to understand that the reward of spending forever in heaven with God was available to those who snapped it up right away *and* to those who came on board at the end. Jammy or what!

STAR STARTER

There are absolutely loads of TV programmes offering people the chance to be famous. It seems that almost everyone wants to be a star these days and they're just waiting for that moment when someone spots them and gives them the big break that they've been hoping for. So, here's a question for you. What would you think if God picked you out of the crowd and said that He was going to make you a household name around the world?

While you have a think about your answer, let me tell you about someone who that actually happened to – and his name was Abram.

Abram (he eventually changed his named to Abraham) had been born in a place called Ur but was now living hundreds of miles away in Haran. Abram's dad (Terah) had uprooted his family and had planned for them to settle in the distant land of Canaan. Unfortunately Terah hadn't made it that far and died in Haran, but the journey wasn't over for his son.

God spoke to Abram (though the Bible doesn't tell you how) and told him to pack his bags and to make tracks for Canaan.

This wasn't because God thought that it would be nice for Abram to have a change of scenery. Here's what was going on. God had chosen him to start a brand-new nation that

was going to change the world! Nothing more, nothing less. How's that for a jammy overnight success?

Sure enough, Abram obeyed God and (with his wife Sarai, his nephew Lot, all the possessions they had accumulated and the people they had acquired in Haran) they set out for the land of Canaan.

Why do you think God chose Abra(ha)m above all the other people of his day? Was it because of his good looks? Was it because he was talented?

The answer is found in Bible book James, chapter 2 and verse 23.

NO CALL-OUT CHARGE

Jesus must have been very fit because He walked almost everywhere He went. He was forever criss-crossing the land of Israel telling people about God and healing sick people. On this occasion, He'd just been to Capernaum where He'd healed the servant of a Roman centurion and had then trekked for the best part of a day down towards the town of Nain.

Wherever Jesus went people followed Him, and this day was no exception. As Jesus entered Nain with a crowd in tow, a funeral procession was going the other way, heading in the direction of the cemetery outside the town.

A young man had died leaving his mum (a widow) all alone. Not only had she lost her son but she'd also lost her means of support. In those days the son would have provided for his parents, but now she was left helpless.

Jesus' heart went out to the poor lady. He went up to the coffin and the men carrying it stopped in their tracks. What on earth was Jesus up to? It was one thing offering your sympathies, but interrupting a funeral procession was well out of order.

Jesus wasn't bothered about things like that. His only concern was to demonstrate that God can change things if we let Him.

To everyone's amazement Jesus called to the young man to come out of the coffin:

'Young man, I say to you, get up!'

Excuse me? He's dead! Surely a dead person is not going to hear that!

Don't ask me how it happened, but at Jesus' command the widow's son sat bolt upright and began to talk.

The Bible says that Jesus gave the young man back to his mother as a free gift from God.

That's what you call a close call. A few minutes later and the fella would have been dead and buried, but now the jammy young man was alive and kicking. How good is that!

Want to find out what happened next?

Check out Bible book Luke, chapter 7 and verses 16 and 17.

13
JAMMY-OLOGY

If you're into fancy words then how about getting your chops around this one?

Genealogy (pronounced JEE-NEE-OLLOW-JEE).

In short it means a record or chart of someone's ancestors. It's a bit like a family tree where you can find out who you are descended from and more to the point, if any of your ancestors were rich or famous.

The Bible quite handily gives us Jesus' family tree right back to Adam (the world's first man) in Bible book Luke, chapter 3 and verses 23 through to 38. And, in Bible book Matthew, chapter 1 from verse 1 through to 17, there's another list of Jesus' ancestors that takes you back not quite so far, to a guy called Abraham who started the Jewish nation to which Jesus belonged.

Why not take a sneaky look for yourself at this second list of who's who in Jesus' family tree?

Here are some fascinating things that you can discover:

First off, not all Jesus' ancestors were Jewish. A gal called Ruth (who was the great grandmum of King David) was a Moabite, which meant she was a foreigner. She married a Jew and when he died she stuck by her ma-in-law (Naomi) and even went so far as to worship her God. God liked that a lot

and gave Ruth another husband, a fella called Boaz. (He's also in Jesus' genealogy.)

Then there was a Canaanite lady called Rahab. Her claim to fame (other than being in Jesus' family tree) was that she hid two Israelite spies in the city of Jericho before Joshua's army invaded it. Her reward was to be spared being put to the sword, along with all her family.

Looks like Rahab fell on her feet, doesn't it?

Whether Ruth and Rahab were jammy in getting into Jesus' family tree or whether God rewarded their faithfulness, who knows? Either way it's brilliant how God is always looking out for more people to join His family.

To find out what I'm talking about head to Bible book Ephesians, chapter 1 and verse 5.

ROTTEN RAIDERS ROUTED

Just for your info, during the course of its history the nation of Israel did the splits and became two nations. One bit was still called Israel and the other was named Judah. Judah had more good kings than Israel, one of whom was Hezekiah.

King Hezekiah stood up for God and went so far as to rebel against the Assyrians who wanted to rule over Israel.

Between you and me the Assyrians were not very pleased about this and a few years later decided to take their revenge.

Sennacherib (king of Assyria) attacked all the fortified cities of Judah and captured the lot of 'em.

Then, King Hezekiah freaked out and offered the Assyrians just about anything they wanted, so long as they backed off.

The cornered king stumped up gold by the bucket load and then stripped Israel's Temple of all its treasures in an attempt to appease Assyria's miffed monarch.

Was that going to be enough to make King Sennacherib turn round and go back the way he'd come? Nope. He was going nowhere.

The Assyrians began to taunt Hezekiah and to make out that he was all alone in the world – not even his Egyptian neighbours or the God he worshipped were going to rescue him.

King Hezekiah tore his clothes and put on sackcloth, which was a sign of how desperate he was. Things were looking bad and the only option left for him was to cry out to God for help.

God heard him loud and clear. God's reply (through the prophet Isaiah) was that the wicked King Sennacherib was going to hear some news that would make him turn tail. Not only that, God was going to have him killed by the sword as well.

Sure enough Sennacherib got wind of the fact that yet another king was on his way to attack the Assyrian army. But that night, before the Assyrians had even broken camp, an angel of God went through their camp and killed 185,000 of them!

Next morning, King Sennacherib and the survivors hot-footed it back to their own land. Phew, that was jammy. What a close one!

Did Sennacherib die by the sword?

Bible book 2 Kings, chapter 19 and verse 37 holds the answer.

PLUNDER BLUNDER

God had chosen a guy called David to replace Saul as king of Israel, but King Saul was none too happy about it. He was out to get David and to kill him before he got anywhere near Israel's throne. So, David, along with 600 fighting men and their families, had to escape to the nearby land of the Philistines and set up home in a place called Ziklag.

This jammy Bible story catches up with David and his men while they were away at war.

The meanie Amalekites (who lived nearby), grabbed their chance and attacked Ziklag, carting everyone off with them.

When David and his men returned they were distraught to find their homes burned to the ground and their families taken captive. The Bible says that they wept until they had no strength left.

The bad news for David was that when their strength did return they were all for stoning him to death. If it hadn't been for David wanting to go to war, none of this would have happened.

At times like these David did what he knew best. He prayed to God.

Should they chase after the Amalekite raiders and attack them or would that end in defeat?

To David's relief it was good news. God told 'em to pursue

the Amalekites because the victory was going to be theirs.

On their way they had a stroke of good fortune. They stumbled across an Egyptian who was ill and in need of food and water. He had been an Amalekite slave and could tell David and his men where to find them.

David plied the poor fellow with food and water and then they all set off in hot pursuit.

The Egyptian was as good as his word and sure enough, before long, they spied the Amalekites.

They were scattered across the countryside eating, drinking and celebrating because of the plunder that they'd nabbed, little suspecting that they were about to be attacked themselves.

And that was their downfall.

David and his band of men fought a bloody battle from dawn to dusk.

Were they victorious? Did his family have a jammy escape?

Look up the answer in Bible book 1 Samuel, chapter 30 and verses 17 to 20.

16
THE EXIT FACTOR

How would you feel if you'd been a slave in a foreign land for yonks and then finally had been given your freedom? Yep, you'd be doing cartwheels, wouldn't you?

So it should come as no surprise to you that a guy called Moses was in the mood for celebrating when he suddenly realised that the Israelite nation had escaped from the clutches of Egypt's nasty Pharaoh.

For hundreds of years God's special people had been held captive in Egypt, but God had heard their cries for help and had sent Moses to rescue them.

It took a lot of persuading to make Pharaoh let hundreds of thousands of Israelite slaves go free. In fact, God unleashed nine terrifying plagues on the Egyptians before he'd finally had enough and relented.

No sooner had the Israelites packed their bags and left than hard-hearted Pharaoh changed his mind and sent his army to fetch them back.

Fortunately he didn't succeed which is why Moses and the Israelites were in a jubilant mood as we drop in on this particular Bible story.

In fact they were in full flow, retelling the details of their jammy escape in a song.

They sang about how God parted the Red Sea so that they could escape but then, how it closed in over the Egyptian army as they followed in hot pursuit.

Here's a flavour of it:

'Pharaoh's chariots and his army
God has hurled into the sea.
The best of Pharaoh's officers
are drowned in the Red Sea.
The deep waters have covered them;
they sank to the depths like a stone.'

Just when the song seemed to be building to a final crescendo, who should jump in but Moses' sister Miriam with a chorus she'd made up herself.

Who were Miriam's backing group and was she any good as a songwriter?

BETWEEN YOU AND ME I THINK THAT MOSES IS SINGING A BIT FLAT!

Go to Bible book Exodus, chapter 15 and verses 20 and 21 to see.

17

KEEP TAKING THE TABLETS

Have you ever wondered what God's handwriting looks like? Well, there's actually a Bible story which features God writing some mysterious words on a wall and there's also a Bible story that tells of when God wrote something called the 'Ten Commandments' on a couple of stone tablets (slabs). And that's the one we're going to look at now.

Moses (the leader of the Israelite nation) had gone up onto Mount Sinai to collect these stone tablets which had ten of God's most important laws written on them. They had been engraved by God's hand on both the front and the back of the slabs.

Moses had been gone quite a while (forty days to be precise) and in the meantime the Israelites had begun to wonder whether they'd ever see him again. Having come to the conclusion that they didn't really care, they decided to give up on the God who had looked after them and to make a god of their own – out of gold.

God was not happy about this at all and nor for that matter was Moses. As soon as he saw what was going on, in a fit of rage, Moses flung the stone tablets to the ground and they broke into smithereens. Gulp!

How crazy was that! Destroying something that God had made with His own hands. What would God say?

Fear not. God wasn't cross with Moses in the least, but something was going to have to be done about those broken Ten Commandments.

Who knows if Moses was any good at jigsaws but there was no way anyone was going to put all the pieces back together again.

There was nothing for it but to make two brand-new tablets.

First time round God had not only written the Ten Commandments but He'd cut the stone slabs as well.

This time God gave Moses the job of chiseling out a couple of stone tablets.

It's not completely clear if it was God or Moses who actually re-wrote the Ten Commandments but, either way, Moses was fortunate that he'd got away with it.

Moses was certainly a jammy wotsit!

When Moses came down from the mountain a second time with the new tablets of stone, do you think he looked a bit sheepish and had his tail between his legs?

Take a look at Bible book Exodus, chapter 34 and verse 29 to find out.

FRIED ALIVE

A lthough Israel's kings were supposed to worship God and be good kings, that wasn't always the case. King Ahaziah was one such rotten ruler.

Ahaziah had fallen through the lattice of a room in his house and had done himself a mischief. He was in a right old bad way and wanted to know what his chances were of recovery. It didn't occur to him to consult the God of Israel to see what He had to say on the matter. Instead he sent some messengers to find out how the god of the people of Ekron (Israel's enemies) rated his chances.

An angel of God had given Elijah (a prophet of God) the heads up on what Ahaziah was up to and he went out to meet the king's messengers.

'Is it because there is no God in Israel that you are going off to consult Baal-Zebub, the god of Ekron?' asked Elijah.

Before they could reply he gave them the news that God's mind was made up on this one and that King Ahaziah would surely die. Gulp!

When the messengers returned to the king he was a bit on edge and wondered why they'd come back so soon. Having told their story, Ahaziah soon twigged that it was Elijah who was behind this and sent one of his army captains out with fifty men to capture the prophet.

Elijah was sitting on a hill but, before they could get anywhere near him, fire fell from heaven and burned the lot of 'em to a cinder.

The king was not going to be put off that easily and sent another fifty men out with another captain to seize Elijah.

Surprise, surprise, the same thing happened again and they were fried alive as well.

When King Ahaziah sent out a third lot of soldiers to get Elijah, the captain of this lot was a little more wary. He fell to his knees and begged the prophet not to burn them up.

Elijah conceded (that was a jammy close shave) and went back with them to the king where he repeated God's decree that Ahaziah would die and not recover.

Did Ahaziah die as Elijah predicted?

MYSTERY MAN

There are a few things people know about a guy who was called Abram. For one thing, they know that he was the founder of the Jewish nation. Another thing they know is that he had his son Isaac when he was one hundred years old, but few people know that our main man was also a bit of a warrior when he needed to be.

Let me explain.

Because God's hand of blessing was on him, Abram very soon became rich and powerful. He had land; he had cattle; he had wealth. Not bad, huh?

His nephew Lot who lived a little distance from him had also done nicely for himself thank you very much, and when Sodom (the place that Lot was living in) was attacked by a bunch of marauding kings, they carried off Lot and his wealth with them.

Abram soon got to hear about the fate of his nephew and set about a daring rescue mission. Along with 318 trained fighters, Abram went in search of Lot. Abram's mini army won the day and Lot was rescued. Hurrah!

But that's not the end of the story. Not only did the grateful king of Sodom come out to greet Lot's victorious uncle, so also did another fella.

His name was Melchizedek and he was the king of Salem.

Next up this mystery man did something a little unusual.

He brought with him bread and wine and then said to Abram, 'I bless you in the name of God Most High, Creator of heaven and earth. All praise belongs to God Most High for helping you defeat your enemies.' Wow!

Abram must have been a bit chuffed because the Bible tells us he gave Melchizedek a tenth of everything.

Not a bad deal for the king of Salem. He gives some bread and wine and in exchange Abram gives him ten per cent of what he has. Nice one, Melchizedek!

Who was the king of Salem? Nobody quite knows. The Bible likens him to someone else you may have heard of.

See if you can work out who it is in Bible book Hebrews, chapter 7 and verses 1 to 3.

USE YOUR LOAF

The Bible is chock-a-block full of stories about God's miracles. Most of the time God used ordinary people to perform them and one such chap was called Elisha (remember him?). He was a prophet and acted as God's mouthpiece in the land of Israel, telling the king what God wanted him to hear and making sure the nation kept on track with God.

Elisha not only said some pretty powerful things but he also did some rather nifty miracles. Once, he provided a widow with an almost never-ending supply of oil which she sold to pay off a debt, and another time, he prevented a bunch of fellow prophets from coming down with a nasty case of food poisoning.

No miracle was too big or too small for Elisha, so he was a good guy to hang around with.

In this Bible story that's just what's going on. Elisha and a hundred men are chilling out. (There's a good chance that they could also have been prophets because we know that Elisha ran a school for prophets.) As we dive into the story, one of Elisha's servants turns up from a place called Baal Shalishah with a bread delivery of twenty yummy fresh loaves.

I'll bet the smell of them made everyone feel peckish.

There was just one small problem, and when I say small, I

mean small. The barley loaves were probably no bigger than the bread rolls we eat nowadays. That was barely enough for a snack for twenty men let alone a full blown, fill-you-up meal for a hundred. What a pickle! (Actually some pickle to go on the bread might have helped.)

Well, that's what Elisha's servant thought anyway. Elisha wasn't fazed at all.

The powerful prophet told the servant that God would sort this one out and to go ahead and share the bread out. Elisha assured him that there would be enough for everyone and even some leftovers.

Was Elisha right or did the servant have to pop to the shops to buy something more filling for the famished fellas?

21

RAINBOW REMINDER

Way back in the mists of time there was a whopping big flood that just about destroyed everything on the planet. Here's what happened.

When God created human beings, He was pleased with the way they'd turned out, but it didn't take long for our distant ancestors to turn their backs on Him and to go their own wicked way. This upset God big time.

There was one guy though who hadn't gone the way of all the others. His name was Noah and he lived a life that pleased God – so much so that God decided that, although He was going to wipe everyone else off the face of the earth because of their wickedness, Noah and his family would be spared. That was a bit jammy for them, wasn't it? Bet they were grateful for a godly dad!

God told Noah to build a huge boat-like box (called an ark), big enough not only to hold his family, but also two of every kind of animal that roamed the earth and soared in the skies. When God's worldwide flood came they'd all be spared.

Sure enough what God promised came to pass and a mahoosive flood of the like the world had never seen before engulfed the entire planet, destroying every land-based creature that wasn't afloat on Noah's ark.

When the flood waters eventually subsided and the ark had come to rest, Noah and his family went out to survey the damage. They were the only survivors and, along with their animal passengers, it was up to them to set about repopulating the world.

But hang on a minute. Supposing the same thing happened again and Noah's descendants also did the dirty on God? Would God bring another flood?

He'd already made His mind up on the matter.

The Bible says that God promised Noah that the world would never again suffer a destructive flood like they'd just lived through. Yes there might be local floods because that's what storms do, but never a worldwide one to wipe away wickedness.

To prove that He was going to be true to His Word, God said that He was going to give people a sign.

Take a look what it was in Bible book Genesis, chapter 9 and verses 12 through to 17.

22
BROTHER BOTHER

Joseph had become the second most important man in Egypt, but it hadn't always been that way. Joseph was one of twelve boys, and most of them didn't like it that he was their dad's blue-eyed boy. As far as they were concerned, the sooner he was out of the way the better. So they sold him into slavery and pretended to their dad (Jacob) that Joseph had been killed by wild animals.

Joseph had ended up in Egypt and after a few ups and downs he found himself promoted to Pharaoh's No. 2. How's that for jammy?

Well, that's not the only jammy thing in this Bible story. When Joseph's long-lost brothers turned up begging for grain because of a terrible famine that had hit that part of the world, he immediately recognised them (although they didn't recognise him). Would Joseph use his powerful position to get his revenge? The Bible says that after throwing them into prison for a few days he sent them on their way with all the grain they needed. What Joseph wanted more than anything was to see his younger brother, Benjamin, and his dad. He said that one of them (Simeon) would be kept in prison until they returned with their youngest brother. He pretended this was a test to see if they were spies.

On their return trip to Egypt for more grain, the brothers brought Benjamin back with them and Simeon was released from prison.

Joseph had one more trick up his sleeve and, after treating them all to a slap up meal, he sent them on their way again, this time with instructions to bring back Jacob.

Joseph also had his favourite silver cup planted in one of their bags of grain without them knowing. As they set off Joseph sent his steward in hot-pursuit to accuse them of stealing the silver cup. Whoever had it was for the chop. Guess whose bag it was in? Benjamin's.

The brothers were desperate and pleaded with Joseph not to kill their youngest brother. One of them even offered to take his place. Did Joseph punish his brothers for the way they had treated him or had they changed their ways?

Check out the jammy ending in Bible book Genesis, chapter 45 and verses 1 through to 15.

MEAT CHEAT

Right from the day that Jacob and Esau (the twins who star in this Bible story) were born, they had been in competition with each other. Although Esau popped out first, Jacob was not far behind him. In fact, he was born grabbing on to Esau's heel!

At the point we catch up with the brothers, Jacob had already managed to trick Esau out of his birthright. This was the wealth and position that Esau, by tradition, would inherit as head of the family. Jammy Jacob!

And now that the time had come for their dad (Isaac) to die, Jacob was still looking for ways to get one over on his older brother.

Isaac knew his days were numbered and summoned Esau to send him out hunting and to bring back wild game for one last meal. After that Isaac would give Esau his blessing. The blessing was a way of passing on, from one person to another, all the good stuff that God wanted to give you. Whoever got this blessing would be set up for life.

Although Esau was Isaac's favourite son, Jacob was the favourite of Isaac's wife, Rebekah. She'd overheard Isaac's last request and had quickly hatched a cunning plan to nab the blessing for Jacob instead. Here's how it all went down.

While Rebekah cooked a meaty meal for Isaac, Jacob disguised himself as Esau with goat skins on his hands and neck to make out he was hairy like his big brother.

Isaac's eyesight was not what it used to be and he fell for the ruse, meaty meal and all.

Jammy Jacob not only had Esau's birthright but he'd now nabbed his blessing as well.

As soon as Jacob got what he'd come for he made a quick exit. And just in the nick of time.

Yikes! Here comes Esau.

Want to find out how the story ends?

TAKE TWO!

I'll bet you've heard of a guy called Moses, haven't you? Although a Hebrew slave by birth, he'd been adopted by an Egyptian princess and brought up in Egypt's royal household. That's what I call jammy! But don't think that's the end of this story. There's more jamminess to come.

The Egyptian king (Pharaoh) was giving his Hebrew slaves a hard time and Moses was having none of it and ended up killing an Egyptian in the process. Oops!

When Pharaoh heard of this he wanted Moses' guts for garters.

Realising his days of luxury were over, Moses did a runner as fast as his legs would carry him. So much for using his position of influence to rescue his people from slavery – it looked like he'd well and truly blown it.

Moses ended up in the back of beyond in the land of Midian. Hopefully Pharaoh wouldn't find him there in the middle of the desert. He had little choice but to settle down and make the best of a bad job.

Moses married a gal called Zipporah and spent his days tending the flocks of his father-in-law, Jethro.

Moses had been forty when he'd scarpered from Egypt and now he'd hit the ripe old age of eighty.

Just when Moses had probably given up all hope of being part of God's rescue plan for the Hebrews in Egypt, God showed up.

Moses had been out with the flocks when God appeared to him in a rather odd way. A bush seemed to be on fire and from it came a voice, which was God's.

The bottom line is that God was giving Moses a second chance to finish what he'd started all those years ago. Now that's what I meant when I said there was more jamminess to come.

Second time around though Moses wasn't quite so keen on the idea. I mean, how was one old man like him going to persuade Egypt's powerful Pharaoh to loosen his iron grip on his Hebrew slaves and let them go free? Come to think of it, what would the Hebrews think of Moses? What was going to persuade them that he was God's man for the moment?

Fear not! God had thought this one through.

You can find out how in Bible book Exodus, chapter 4 and verses 1 to 8.

JUMPED-UP JOSHUA?

oor old Moses. He'd led the Israelites out of slavery in Egypt, he'd stuck with them for forty years in the desert after they'd rebelled against God, and now God wasn't going to let him lead them into the land of Canaan which He'd given them as a place to settle in.

To be fair to God, it was Moses' fault. When the Israelites were grumbling about how thirsty they were and God told Moses to speak to a rock to release water, Moses whacked it twice because he was cheesed off with their moaning. For God's part, He was upset that Moses had not done what He'd commanded. The price for his disobedience was God not allowing him to enter Canaan.

On the plus side, God did let Moses go up on a mountain to take a peek at the land before he died.

With Moses having to let go of the reins of leading the Israelites, they needed a new man at the helm to lead them into God's promised land. This was no time for putting a 'situation vacant' ad in the paper and doing job interviews. God already knew who He'd lined up to step into Moses' shoes (or perhaps I should say, sandals).

The only guy in the frame, as far as God was concerned, was a fella called Joshua.

Who knows if the Israelites wondered how jammy Joshua had managed to get into God's good books and land the top job in the land? God certainly did though, and to His way of thinking, Israel's new leader most certainly wasn't a jumped-up Joshua.

Joshua had lived through their nation's deliverance from slavery in Egypt; he'd been one of the twelve spies to spy out Canaan many years before, and he'd endured forty years in the desert with his fellow Israelites who didn't agree with him that they should go and conquer the land then and there. Joshua had spent loads of his spare time in the tabernacle tent where he went to take time out with God and to worship Him.

Plus, for many years Joshua had been acting as Moses' assistant.

So Joshua had learned all he needed to know about leading the Israelites from Moses and all about how to keep the Israelites on track with God, from God.

Check out Bible book Numbers, chapter 27 and verses 18 to 23 to read the end of this story.

26
CLOSE CALL SAUL

King Saul of Israel was on the warpath for a guy called David, whom God had lined up to replace him (as king). Saul was having none of it and wanted David dead and buried.

David and his men had to resort to hiding out in the desert but there seemed to be no escape from Saul and his 3,000 troops. Before long they were hot on David's trail. As Saul and his men made camp, David sent out scouts to check if it really was Saul that he'd spied in the distance. Yep, it sure was.

Creeping up closer to get a better view of his foe, David saw that the king was fast asleep with his men all around him. David asked for volunteers to go with him down into their camp. Abishai was up for it – so off the pair went.

It was the dead of night and they found Saul sound asleep with his spear plonked in the ground beside his head and his soldiers lying around him. David and Abishai didn't think much of the king's armed guard but did they make the most of their opportunity? No, they didn't. This was Saul's jammy day.

Abishai was all for skewering King Saul with one lunge of the spear but David knew better.

As far as he was concerned Saul was still the anointed king in God's eyes, even though his days were numbered. To kill the king would be to go against God, and David wasn't going to do that.

Instead they quietly took the spear, and also a water jug from beside Saul, and tip-toed away while their enemies slept.

Once back to safety, David called out at the top of his voice to taunt the men who were supposed to be guarding their king. He told them that they deserved the death penalty for failing to stop him and Abishai venturing into their camp so brazenly, and then taking Saul's spear and water jar.

Saul woke up with all the commotion. He knew that voice from somewhere. Yep, it was David. Where was the rotter?

David told Saul of their daring night raid and how he'd spared the king's life because he respected him.

Did King Saul rally his troops and go after David, despite all of that?

NO, LEAVE THE TEDDY BEAR!

Find your answer in Bible book 1 Samuel, chapter 26 and verse 25.

27

AN EYE-OPENER

The king of Aram was in a bit of a pickle. Every time he went to attack Israel, God warned Israel's king what he was up to. God's message boy in all of this was none other than (yep, you've guessed it) wonderman, prophet Elisha.

First off, the king of Aram thought that it was an inside job, and that one of his own people was leaking top secret information to the Israelites. He demanded to know who the traitor was, but everyone denied having anything to do with it.

When Aram's angry king found out from them that Elisha was the culprit, he set out to put an end to the prophet's underhand antics, once and for all.

Word soon reached the king's ears that Elisha was in a place called Dothan, so he dispatched an army to capture him.

The king's chariots and horses surrounded the city by night. Next morning Dothan's inhabitants woke up to a bit of a shock!

Elisha's servant was terrified but the prophet was as calm as a cucumber.

He trusted God to protect them so he knew for certain that the place would be swarming with angels. His servant needed a little convincing though, so Elisha prayed to God that he'd be able to see them. The servant got more than he bargained

for. He saw the hills absolutely jam-packed with horses and chariots of fire protecting them.

As the king of Aram's troops advanced, Elisha shot up a prayer to God to strike them all blind.

And that's exactly what happened.

The Bible says that Elisha went out and told them that they'd got the wrong place.

His plan was to lead them to Samaria where the king of Israel resided.

So Elisha led the blind army into Samaria and then, God opened their eyes again.

Did the king of Israel put his captive enemy to the sword?

Check out Bible book 2 Kings, chapter 6 and verses 21 to 23 to read about a really jammy ending.

28

TEN MEN

J esus was to-ing and fro-ing across Israel, healing people and telling them about God.

In this Bible story Jesus is making tracks for Jerusalem and on the way He had to pass along the border between Samaria and Galilee.

As Jesus entered a village he met ten men suffering with leprosy.

According to the Jewish religion, if you had this particular skin disease you had to steer well clear of everyone else. You were what was known as 'unclean', and towns and villages were most definitely off limits. Lepers lived in the hillsides and begged for food. It was bad enough having to live with the leprosy but a double whammy being an outcast as well.

But Jesus didn't take any notice of those rules and regulations. He cared for people too much to keep them at a distance, and these lepers were no exception.

My guess is that they must have known a thing or two about Jesus, because they called out to Him to have pity on them.

It's pretty clear that they were expecting something more from Jesus than their next meal.

Jesus seemed to pick up on this. The Bible says that He *did* have pity on them.

It's absolutely amazing but Jesus didn't actually pray for these poor guys. He simply told these jammy fellas to show themselves to the local priests.

According to their customs you only went to the priest like this if you wanted your healing confirmed. The priest would be the one to say that they weren't unclean any more.

The lepers all put their trust in Jesus to be healed but one of them stood out from the crowd. He wasn't actually a Jew himself but a Samaritan. As far as Jews were concerned Samaritans had no part in their religion.

Although this man wasn't part of their nation he did something awesome.

29
JAMMY JERUSALEM

In this jammy Bible story we're going to take a look at some awesome stuff that was going on soon after the world's first church was started. It was in a place called Jerusalem, not long after Jesus had returned to heaven.

Before He went, Jesus handed over to His followers the job of carrying on where He'd left off. This meant telling people that Jesus had taken the punishment for all the wrong stuff they'd done – which made it possible for them to be friends with God again. As the icing on the cake, and to prove God was for real, His followers were given the power and authority to perform the same sort of miracles that Jesus did while He was on earth.

The Bible says that this was precisely what the apostles (the twelve main leaders of this first church) were up to, as we drop in on them.

Such was the impact these guys were making that the church just grew and grew. There were thousands of them, so finding a building to fit in was a non-starter. That's why they hung out in what was called Solomon's Colonnade. Although these believers in Jesus had a fantastic reputation, the people who were not part of their number kept their distance. I guess they were a bit awestruck by the amazing miracles and didn't quite know what to make of it all.

That didn't stop people becoming followers of Jesus though, and the church just kept on growing and growing.

One thing's for sure, people wanted what this power-packed church had to offer and flocked to the apostles with their sick. It didn't matter how the sick got there – be it on beds or mats – just so long as they did. The atmosphere was buzzing with so much expectation that they believed even the shadow of Peter (one of the apostles) just passing over sick people, would be enough to heal them.

It wasn't only the jammy inhabitants of Jerusalem who hit the jackpot by having these miracle-working guys on their doorstep. Distance was no object and crowds swarmed in from the towns around Jerusalem as well. The Bible says that everyone got healed.

But not everyone was kicking their heels with joy at what was going on.

Find out what I mean in Bible book Acts, chapter 5 and verses 17 and 18.

30

SNEAKY SNARE

When it came to celebrities Jesus was about as big as you were going to get in His day. Not that He was the least bit interested in fame and acclaim, but just about everywhere Jesus went, crowds clamoured around Him.

One particular day Jesus made an appearance outside the Temple in Jerusalem. It might have only been the crack of dawn but a crowd had already gathered to hear what He had to say and to see what He would do. (When Jesus was around you never knew quite what to expect.) The Bible says that Jesus sat down and began to teach the people.

Suddenly there was a big kerfuffle and the meeting was abruptly disrupted by a bunch of religious leaders intent on getting one over on Jesus. With them was a woman who'd been caught getting up to some hanky panky with a man who wasn't her husband. The religious leaders made her stand in front of the crowd while they set about putting Jesus on the spot.

They didn't like Jesus one little bit because at every turn He challenged their way of doing things. For His part Jesus accused them of making up so many religious rules and regulations that most folks had long given up hope of getting to know God. Instead of being a gateway to God, the religious leaders were like a brick wall, and Jesus said so.

Bringing the woman that they'd caught in adultery to Jesus was actually a trap to catch Him out. Jewish law said that the penalty for her crime was to be stoned to death. The religious leaders knew that Jesus was merciful and compassionate and wouldn't want that to happen, but they also knew that as a Jew He should abide by their law. If they could just discredit Him then they would have won.

OK, so Jesus did respect God's laws, but He'd come to earth to show people a better way to live that wasn't about punishment, it was about mercy. Jesus wanted to show people that He could help them live lives that pleased God, not because they had to but because they wanted to.

How did Jesus get out of the pickle He seemed to be in? He just said one simple statement to the religious leaders. 'If any of you is without sin, let him be the first to throw a stone at her.'

Did the woman have a jammy escape?

Hurry off to Bible book John, chapter 8 and check out verses 9 to 11 pronto.

31

A QUICK EXIT

When the Church first kicked off in Jerusalem a couple of thousand years ago, it seemed like everyone was doing awesome things in God's power.

The guy in this Bible story (Philip) was part of a team who made sure that anyone who was hard up didn't go hungry. OK, so Philip might have worked in the food distribution department, but that didn't stop him telling people about Jesus and doing miracles.

One day Philip had a heads-up from an angel of God to make tracks for the desert road that led out of Jerusalem, so off he went. On his way Philip met a top bod who worked for the queen of faraway Ethiopia. The official (who was travelling in a chariot) happened to be checking out some stuff from the Jewish Scriptures but was a bit puzzled as to what it all meant.

At a word from God, Philip raced after the chariot and then jogged beside it. Philip asked the chap if he had any idea what he was reading. He hadn't a clue. So, without further ado (and probably before he ran out of puff) Philip climbed up into the chariot. Philip explained that the book was all about Jesus and how He'd made it possible for everyone (that includes us today) to be friends with God.

The Ethiopian didn't need much persuading and made his

mind up there and then to become a follower of Jesus. To seal the deal he asked Philip if he could be baptised. What's that when it's at home?

I'll tell you. To demonstrate to God and others that you've turned your back on living life for yourself and are now living one hundred per cent for God, you can be baptised by the Church. It simply means being submerged in water and then lifted back up again (a bit like when in some churches, babies are baptised – but in this case *you're* making the decision, not your parents).

So that's what they did. Finding some water, Philip baptised the Ethiopian.

Now I'll bet that riding along that desert road wasn't the most comfortable experience but Philip didn't have to worry about that. Jammy Philip was about to get the gold star treatment from God …

I t's always quite nice to be singled out for special attention, isn't it? So how would you feel if God had you at the top of His list for special treatment?

Well, that's just what happened to the jammy people of Macedonia in this Bible story. Let me fill you in on the details.

A guy called Paul had been making his way around the Mediterranean region telling people about Jesus and how He had made it possible for us to have a fresh start in life with God.

There was absolutely no stopping Paul. Nowhere was off limits for this feisty fella. Paul had the bit between his teeth and would go just about anywhere to spread the great news about Jesus.

Paul travelled huge distances by foot or by boat to get the message out, risking danger and hardship in the process. Along the way he was shipwrecked three times, beaten with rods and stoned. He went without food, was cold, went without sleep, spent a night and a day in the open sea … (phew!) and loads more! Being on the road for Jesus was definitely no picnic.

Fortunately for Paul, God was with him every step of the way, protecting him, encouraging him and also directing him where he should go.

Hold your horses! Did I just say God directed him? Yep, I did. So how on earth did God do that? Did Paul have a map

or better still his very own sat nav? Well, I don't know about the map but one thing's for sure, he didn't have a sat nav.

Although Paul was happy to go anywhere and everywhere, God sometimes had different ideas. It wasn't that Paul was wrong, it was just that there were some people who needed to hear about Jesus before others. Whenever God wanted Paul to make a detour He'd often as not send either an angel to redirect him or have His Holy Spirit (the One who God called our Guide and Counsellor) intervene.

The Holy Spirit had already just temporarily prevented Paul from travelling into Bithynia and the province of Asia. Why? Well, during the night, Paul had received a vision of a man from Macedonia begging him to come over to help them. Oh, so that was the reason.

To see how this story ended look in Bible book Acts, chapter 16 and verses 10 through to 15.

WELL JAMMY

33

There's an expression that talks about being in the right place at the right time. That's what happened to the woman who stars in this Bible story.

We don't know her name but we do know that she lived in a town called Sychar in Samaria. Jesus was heading back to Galilee and was passing through her neck of the woods.

It was around the middle of the day and Jesus was flaked out after walking in the heat. Time to put His feet up and rest His weary legs while His disciples popped into town to grab some lunch.

Jesus plonked Himself down by a well and waited. Meanwhile a local lady rocked up to get some water. She had absolutely no idea who Jesus was but this chance meeting (though I reckon God had set it up good and proper) with God's Son was going to change the life of this jammy woman for good.

To the lady's surprise Jesus asked her for a drink.

The reason it was a surprise is that Jews (and Jesus was one) made it their business not to have anything to do with Samaritans (which this lady was). But Jesus wasn't bothered with that sort of thing. He was happy to get along with anyone.

Jesus didn't miss a trick, and because they were by a well He began to talk to the woman about how He could give her living water. He said that if she drank water from the well she'd be thirsty again but if she drank the water that He was offering she never would.

Jesus was talking about the life-giving Holy Spirit He gives to those who follow Him.

While she was still trying to get her head around what Jesus had been saying, He told her to go fetch her husband.

The woman didn't actually have a husband and she told Jesus so. He knew that! In fact He also knew that she'd had five husbands in the past. She was living with a man right now but they weren't married. Jesus told her all this and she was amazed! Only a man sent from God could know such things, so she hurried back into town to tell everyone about Jesus.

Did they believe her?

34

MAT MAN

Before Jesus' time, sick or disabled people often stood little or no chance of getting better. One last resort was a pool in Jerusalem called Bethesda. It was believed that every now and then an angel of God would drop by to stir up the water and the first person to get in then, would get well. Day after day the blind, the lame and the paralysed waited patiently round the edge of the pool hoping for their miracle. So desperate were they to get better that the place was positively heaving with people.

Who knows if Jesus had been to the pool of Bethesda before but one particular day, when He was in Jerusalem for a Jewish feast, Jesus passed that way.

The Bible tells us that one man there had been an invalid for thirty-eight long years and with apparently no sign of being healed any time soon.

The man explained to Jesus that he had attempted to climb down into the pool when it was stirred up but, without anyone to give him a helping hand, he kept getting pipped to the post by someone quicker.

Having found out this info, Jesus then went and asked him an astonishing question:

'Do you want to get well?'

Hello! Are you serious, Jesus? The poor guy had been an invalid for the best part of forty years and You ask him if he wants to get better!

To all intents and purposes it sounded like Jesus was being really harsh but if you knew anything about the nature of Jesus then you'd know that this just couldn't be true.

The only other option is that Jesus knew something about the man that we don't. Because He's God's Son there's every chance of that being the case.

As if there was any doubt as to Jesus' compassion, He told the man to get up and to pick up his mat (that he was lying on).

Amazingly the chap did what Jesus said and got to his feet. He was instantly healed! Call that jammy, call it a miracle but whatever way you look at it, he could walk.

Not everyone was thrilled though.

Discover who that was in Bible book John, chapter 5 and verse 10.

35
DEATH DEFYING DISCIPLES

You'd think that if a sick person was healed by God everyone would be really pleased. Not so. The apostles (the twelve leaders of the world's first church in Jerusalem) had been having ginormous success in healing people with the power and authority that Jesus had given them. As a result people were becoming followers of Jesus in their droves.

This didn't please Jerusalem's religious leaders one little bit. Jesus (God's Son) had been a thorn in their side while He'd been alive and they thought they'd heard the last of Him when He'd been executed. Now, the religious leaders were well jealous of the apostles who seemed to be carrying on where Jesus had left off and they tried to shut them up by chucking them in jail. That didn't work. An angel of God simply came along at night and unlocked the doors for them. Next morning when the religious leaders sent for the apostles they were nowhere to be found.

What a shock to discover that they were once again back in the Temple courts and refusing to be silenced.

Grrr! The religious leaders were furious and ordered their arrest again. Time to put a stop to their antics once and for all.

When Peter (one of the apostles) gave them a lecture about

who Jesus was, it made them see red. So much so that they wanted to put the lot of 'em to death.

To be fair, they weren't all hot heads. One of the religious leaders (a guy called Gamaliel) had a few things to say on the matter. He had the apostles put outside and then gave his take on things.

If these guys were from God then trying to stop them was a big mistake. On the other hand if they weren't then it would all eventually just fizzle out.

Thanks to Gamaliel the jammy apostles weren't put to death. Did the religious leaders heed Gamaliel's wise words of warning? Not really!

36

JOPPA JOY

Peter used to be a fisherman around the Sea of Galilee but now, a few years on, he was one of the main men in Jerusalem's church. Peter was on his travels and had dropped in on some Christians over to the east of Jerusalem in Lydda. There he came across a chap called Aeneas (pronounced EE-NEE-US) who'd been paralysed and bed-bound for eight years. Peter had seen enough of God's healing power first hand to know that nothing is impossible for God. Peter told Aeneas that Jesus Christ heals him and to get up and tidy his mat. Sure enough the guy was healed and as a result everyone in Lydda (and also in another place called Sharon) became Christians. Oh yes, and Aeneas also tidied up his mat. (I guess that after eight years it must have been mega messy!)

Meanwhile, in nearby Joppa (on the coast), a lady called Tabitha had fallen ill and died. The Bible says that Tabitha had a reputation for helping the poor and doing good. She would be sorely missed.

When the jammy followers of Jesus discovered that none other than Peter was in the area, they sent word for him to come. Peter was taken to an upstairs room where the poor lady's body had been laid. Her friends were distraught. They showed Peter all the robes and clothing that Tabitha had made as they

wept and wailed. There was no way that Peter could concentrate with their tearful din droning on in the background so he sent them out of the room. Peter sank to his knees and prayed to God. Then he turned to Tabitha and commanded the dead lady to get up. Hang on a minute. How was that going to happen? Tabitha was long gone and there's no way she would have been able to hear a word of what Peter was saying.

That didn't matter. God was listening in on Peter's prayer and He was ready and willing to act on it. Tabitha opened her eyes and sat up. Bet she was surprised! Not half as much as her friends when Peter presented her to them alive again.

Take a look in Bible book Acts, chapter 9 and verse 42 to see the impact this miracle had in Joppa.

37

ROCKET MAN

Watching a space rocket leave the launch pad and shoot skyward at a rate of knots is a brilliant sight. But imagine seeing a human being doing something similar. Impossible you say? Well, how about I tell you a Bible story that might change your mind.

It happened around the time that Jesus had been raised from the dead (brought back to life by God) after being executed on a wooden cross. At this point Jesus now had a new body that looked and felt human but could also come and go like the body of an angel. Wow!

Jesus had appeared in His heaven-and-earth-type body to hundreds of His followers over a period of forty days after His resurrection but now, His time on earth was just about up. Jesus was packing His bags (not literally of course) and getting ready to go back to heaven where He'd originally come from.

First though, Jesus was having a meal with His disciples (that's the bunch of guys who would carry on from Him when He'd left) and during it He gave them their final instructions.

Top of the list was that on no account were they to leave Jerusalem (where they were based) until they had been filled with God's Holy Spirit. The plan was that once Jesus had returned to heaven He'd send the Holy Spirit to take over from Him back on earth.

Everything Jesus did He did in God's power, and it was going to be no different for His disciples. A little while back Jesus had told His team that they would do the same things that He had; miracles, healings, bringing the dead back to life. Without the power of the Holy Spirit this was going to be a complete non-starter! Only God can do that sort of stuff, and they knew it.

After telling His disciples that not only would they be power-packed witnesses in Jerusalem, but that He planned for them to go and tell the whole world about Him, Jesus did something amazing! And that was when His jammy disciples got to see the spectacular sight I was talking about at the beginning.

38

ROAD TO RECOVERY

Jesus might have been popular with the crowds who followed Him around (when He lived on earth) but the Jewish religious leaders hadn't taken a shine to Him at all.

They were forever trying to trick Jesus into saying something that was against their religious laws.

On one such occasion, having said that loving God one hundred per cent and loving your neighbour one hundred per cent is what God expects of us, an expert in the law asked Jesus to explain who exactly our neighbour is.

So Jesus told a story about a Jewish man who was on his way from Jerusalem to Jericho. It was not the safest route to take at the best of times and sure enough the poor fella got mugged by a band of rotten robbers. They stripped off his clothes, beat him to a pulp and left him for dead. Fortunately help was at hand, or so he thought. Along the lonely road strolled a Jewish priest. He worked for God full-time (in Jerusalem's Temple) so you'd reckon that he'd be sure to come to the rescue. Nope! Jesus said that the priest crossed to the other side of the road not wanting to get involved.

All was not lost. As the priest slunk off into the distance a Jewish Levite came into view. Maybe this guy would help out.

If you've heard this story before you'll not be shocked to

discover that this Levite (who also worked full-time for God in Jerusalem's Temple) did the same thing. On clapping his eyes on the beaten-up traveller he also made a beeline for the other side of the road and pretended not to notice. What a rotter!

Just when the poor guy was probably about to give up all hope of ever being rescued, a Samaritan appeared. (That's the jammy bit by the way.)

For your info, Jews and Samaritans were not exactly best buddies. The Jewish people didn't think much of their near neighbours and the feeling was no doubt mutual.

When the Samaritan stopped and bent down to tend the guy's wounds no one was more surprised than the journeying Jew himself.

Having cleaned his wounds the Samaritan took the injured man on his donkey to an inn to recover. Not only that but the kind man even footed the bill.

So, according to Jesus, who is our neighbour?

Get stuck into Bible book Luke, chapter 10 and verses 36 through to 37.

39

HE SAW ESAU

I f you know anything about God you'll know that He often chooses the most unlikely people to do great things for Him. One such person was a guy called Jacob. In fact, later in life he had his name changed to Israel – so now a whole nation is called after him.

Jacob's early days were not quite so grand. He had cheated his big brother, Esau, out of his inheritance and scarpered, sharpish, to another land. Now, having settled there, got married, had kids and grandchildren and accumulated vast numbers of animals, he was finally heading home to the land of his birth.

In all these years Jacob had made no effort to patch up his differences with Esau and as he got nearer to home Jacob began to have an attack of the collie-wobbles. What if Esau was still livid? His brother had always been a bit of a tough nut and supposing he took his revenge on Jacob … It didn't bear thinking about.

Although Jacob had made a bit of a mess of things he was still a man who put God first. As a result God had promised that Jacob would be the leader of Israel (not that it was called that yet).

Jacob sent messengers ahead of him to Esau to let his

brother know that he was coming and hoping that bygones would be bygones.

When they returned with the news that Esau was on his way with four hundred men, Jacob was absolutely terrified. He'd been hoping that Esau would bury the hatchet ... but not in him!

Jacob had to think on his feet. What to do? Ah yes, that was it. He'd send Esau gifts of flocks of animals. That ought to pacify his brother.

He split them into three groups so that he would have three shots at appeasing Esau.

Finally the big day arrived and Jacob flung himself on the ground as Esau approached.

Does this story have a jammy ending for Jacob?

Look it up in Bible book Genesis, chapter 33 and verses 4 to 11.

40

DREAM JOB

Joseph was an Israelite who lived in Egypt. He'd arrived there as a slave a few years back and had done pretty well for himself by becoming second-in-command to Egypt's Pharaoh, their all-powerful ruler. How did that happen? Well, to cut a long story short, Pharaoh had a couple of weird dreams but he hadn't a clue what they meant. His magicians and his wise men were none the wiser either. (Sorry about the pun.) One of Pharaoh's servants suddenly remembered a guy he'd spent some time in prison with who was spot on when it came to interpreting dreams.

Without further ado Pharaoh had the man in question (Joseph) brought before him to do his stuff. Having explained that his ability to tell you what a dream meant was from God, Joseph set about interpreting the dreams. God showed Joseph that they both actually meant one and the same thing. Seven years of plenty would be followed by seven years of famine. Two dreams meant that it was fixed and nothing could change that.

Pharaoh was so relieved to have the dreams interpreted that he promptly promoted our Joe to his No. 2. How cool is that?

But that still left Pharoah with the question of what to do about the seven-year famine. That was a long time to go without food. If he didn't act fast, Egypt would be wiped out.

Joseph piped up and suggested that they put someone in charge who was both wise and discerning. He also suggested that Pharaoh appoint commissioners over the land to take twenty per cent of the harvest each year for the seven abundant years and store it away.

Pharaoh thought it was a brilliant idea. Now all they needed was someone to head this up.

It was a no-brainer. Joseph fitted the bill perfectly and sure enough Pharaoh handed him the job.

Everything happened just like God had said. For seven years Joseph made sure that Egypt's stores of grain were so plentiful that the Bible says that it was like the sand of the sea.

How jammy was that for the Egyptians to have Joseph living among them!

Check out what happened when the famine came in Bible book Genesis, chapter 41 and verses 53 and 54.

41
SMASH AND GRAB

God had hand-picked a young man called David to replace Saul as king of Israel. Saul had also been chosen by God but along the way he'd made a bit of a mess of things.

To make matters worse King Saul didn't want to go quietly and did his level best to make sure that David never got within a million miles of Israel's throne! The good news (for David) is that the conniving king didn't have his way. Saul was killed in battle and so the way was open for David to become Israel's rightful ruler.

The tribes of Israel all came to David and pledged their allegiance to him.

And at a place called Hebron, David was anointed Israel's new king. So what's jammy about that you may ask? Nothing yet, but be patient.

Next up King David needed somewhere from which to rule. He was going to be Israel's main man for forty years (not that he knew that, obviously) so he needed a royal city. Jerusalem seemed like as good a place as any and off David and his men went. They couldn't just move in like you can with a house move. There were still people (the Jebusites) living in Jerusalem so there was the small matter of attacking the place first before David could set up shop.

The Jebusites didn't seem too bothered about the presence of an invading army camping outside their fortified city. They even went so far as to taunt them that they were wasting their time. As far as the Jebusites were concerned David's men were no match for them.

It seems like they spoke a little too soon. That very day, after a bit of a scrap, King David took up residence in Jerusalem.

Just to rub salt into the Jebusites' wounds, David decided to call it the City of David. Nice one, David!

He then set about strengthening the city against attack.

Now, if you were a king (like David) and you'd just nabbed yourself a city to rule from, the icing on the cake had to be having a palace, right?

It looks like jammy King David had friends in the right places.

42

KING COPS IT

One of Israel's worst ever kings was a guy called Ahab. His biggest mistake was to worship the gods of his wife, Jezebel. Ahab was spoiling for a fight and when he remembered that one of his towns (the one called Ramoth Gilead) was in the hands of the Arameans he asked the king of Judah (Jehoshaphat) to come with him to fight them.

Having said yes, King Jehoshaphat suggested that it might be worth having a word with God first to see if He thought that waging war was a good idea. Ahab agreed but his idea of consulting with God was to call together the prophets of the gods that he worshipped.

This wasn't really what Jehoshaphat had in mind so he asked if perhaps there was a prophet of God (not Ahab's false gods) thereabouts. Sure there was. He was called Micaiah but he never had anything good to say about Ahab. No wonder the king hated him. Reluctantly Ahab called for Micaiah. All of Ahab's prophets were prophesying victory and success for their king so Micaiah was encouraged to do likewise. Micaiah was happy to oblige and told King Ahab to attack because he would be victorious.

Ahab knew that the prophet was just telling him what his itching ears wanted to hear and ordered Micaiah to tell the truth.

OK, so the truth was that Ahab's army would suffer a terrible defeat.

King Ahab was well miffed with this and had Micaiah thrown into prison with instructions to give him only bread and water until he returned.

Micaiah made it clear that if the king ever returned then God had not spoken through him.

Ahab was obviously jittery when he went into battle and to avoid getting picked out by enemy archers he disguised himself so as not to look like a king.

The wicked king's end might not have been very jammy for him but it was for one of the Aramean archers.

See what I mean in Bible book 1 Kings, chapter 22 and verses 34 to 36.

43

MEAL DEAL

This Bible story is a bit jammy but it's also a bit barmy.

David (Israel's future king) was living out in the open countryside with his trusty band of 400 fighting men. They'd been hanging out in the Desert of Maon on the run from King Saul (Israel's present king). David was a good sort of guy and he made it his business to protect the flocks and servants of a nearby wealthy man called Nabal.

Working out in the open could be dangerous so it was good to have David and his men acting as their bodyguards. In return for their kindness to his servants and flocks David thought that it would be a kind gesture if Nabal would give them food and drink. David sent a message to the wealthy landowner asking for this.

What I haven't told you is that Nabal was a bit of an awkward so-and-so. Well, actually the Bible calls him mean and surly. Either way he was a nasty piece of work and he didn't take too kindly to David's request. Who was this David anyway? Pah! Why should he share his food with this complete stranger? Forget it!

I have to say that David did not take Nabal's rebuttal too kindly. That was no way to repay him. Strapping their swords on, David and his men set off to teach Nabal a lesson he wouldn't forget. When Nabal's wife (Abigail) found out what her foolish husband had done and that David was on the warpath she flew into action.

Abigail gathered as much food as she could and sent her servants ahead with it. Without telling Nabal she rode out to meet David and not only to give him the food that he had asked for but to say sorry for her hubbie's stupidity.

Abigail was intelligent and beautiful and David accepted her apology and made a deal not to bring death and destruction to her household after all. That was a close one!

Nabal knew nothing of this nor did he ever find out, because the next day his heart stopped and he died.

Want to find out the jammy ending for Abigail?

WHO ARE YOU CALLING MEAN AND SURLY?

You'll find it in Bible book 1 Samuel, chapter 25 and verses 39 to 43.

Wicked King Ahab of Israel had recently died and his son Joram had succeeded him as king. To be honest Joram was a chip off the old block and he really wasn't much better than his dastardly dad.

While Ahab had been on the throne, Mesha (king of Moab) had been forced to provide him with thousands of sheep and thousands of wool fleeces. With Ahab now gone the Moabite king decided that enough was enough and it was time to rebel against Israel. Joram was having none of it and persuaded Judah's king (Jehoshaphat) to fight with him against King Mesha. As if you haven't had to get your head round enough kings already, I need to let you know that the king of Edom also joined Joram and Jehoshaphat.

Off they set to fight King Mesha but, after a seven-day march through the Desert of Edom, disaster struck; their drinking water ran out. With thousands of troops and animals to supply this was not good.

Joram blamed God but level-headed Jehoshaphat asked if there was a prophet of God who could help them. Someone suggested Elisha so off they toddled to pay him a visit.

If it hadn't been for Jehoshaphat (who he respected) Elisha

wouldn't have given Joram the time of day. Elisha agreed to find out from God what He had to say.

God told them to dig ditches in the valley where they were camped and then He would fill them with water ... without a drop of rain falling!

Lo and behold, next morning, there it was – water flowing from the direction of Edom and filling up the ditches.

The Moabites knew that an attack was imminent but when they looked across to the three kings' camp, the early morning sun was shining on the water and it looked blood red. They thought that the kings had fought against each other and that the reflection was their blood. It was only as they charged towards the camp that they realised they'd jumped to the wrong conclusion. Joram's army fought back and won the day. Not only had God given them water but He'd also given them a jammy victory as an added bonus.

See how they finished the job in Bible book 2 Kings, chapter 3 and verses 24 to 27.

45
JUST THE TICKET

Old people are often told that it's never too late to try new things. Proof of that in the Bible was a guy called Abraham (and his wife Sarah) who had a kid when he was one hundred and she was ninety. Even when it comes to being friends with God it's never too late.

The Bible makes it clear that even though we might give up on God, He never gives up on us. God's plan is for everyone to be in His family, with absolutely no exceptions. That's why Jesus was sent to planet earth to take the punishment for all the bad stuff we do. And it was God who made the first move to put things right between us and Him because God knew that if He didn't, then nothing would change.

This well-known Bible story tells us about the final moments of Jesus' life but it also tells us about a rather jammy man who got his ticket to heaven right at the last minute.

Jesus had been nailed to a wooden cross by the Romans and left hanging there to die. Down below some people were jeering at Him saying that, if He really was the Son of God why didn't He come down off the cross? They hadn't a clue that Jesus had deliberately chosen to do this for them (and us too). Others, who were close friends of Jesus, simply looked on and wept.

On crosses either side of Jesus hung two criminals.

One on the right and one on the left.

As if he didn't have enough to think about as he hung there in agony, one of them began to join in the taunting and to hurl insults at Jesus as well.

'Aren't You the Christ? Then save Yourself and us!'

The other criminal wasn't such a hot-head and rebuked him.

He pointed out that the pair of them were getting their come-uppance. They deserved to be punished. But not Jesus. He wasn't guilty of any wrongdoing.

Recognising his need of someone to save him, the man turned to Jesus and asked Him to remember him when He came into His kingdom.

It looks like this man had worked out that Jesus was God's Son, doesn't it?

How did Jesus reply?

Look it up in Bible book Luke, chapter 23 and verse 43.

NAME DROPPERS

I n this book you may have already come across a
story about a guy called Joseph who was promoted to
Pharaoh's No. 2 and who was given the authority to act on
the Egyptian ruler's behalf. Whatever Joseph said, it was as if
Pharaoh were saying it himself.

Imagine what it would be like if God gave someone that
same sort of authority. Well, that's exactly what happened to
seventy-two jammy men in this Bible story. Jesus already had
a tip-top team of twelve guys who went around with Him
and they were called His disciples. But there was plenty to
do and it was now time for Jesus to train up some more guys
to make sure things got done. Jesus (if you didn't know it
already) was God's Son, so when He gave these seventy-two
new recruits authority to do stuff in His name it meant that
they could do anything and everything that Jesus did. How
amazing was that!

Jesus had been criss-crossing the land of Israel teaching people
about God and showing God's power in healings and miracles.

This intrepid band of seventy-two men were going to be
Jesus' advance party. Their job was to go on ahead of Him
into the towns and villages to tell people that God was on the
move and to get themselves ready to welcome Him with open

arms. To prove that Jesus was for real the seventy-two were told to heal the sick in Jesus' name, which is simply another way of saying that they were acting on His authority.

These new recruits had been instructed to travel light so they relied upon the inhabitants of the towns and villages to give them food and lodging.

If the welcome mat was not put out to them they had permission to make it clear that God didn't take too kindly to people rejecting His Son, Jesus.

Did having Jesus' authority make a blind bit of difference to the seventy-two Jesus picked?

Find out in Bible book Luke, chapter 10 and verse 17.

MANIC MARTHA

How some brothers and sisters bicker! Jesus got to know a couple of sisters called Mary and Martha. OK, so this Bible story doesn't actually say that the pair of them were at each others' throats, but it seems like they both had different ways of doing things and I guess that would sometimes cause a wee bit of tension around the home.

For instance, in the story I'm about to tell you, Jesus had just rocked up to their village. It was a place called Bethany and although it doesn't tell you so in this story, Mary and Martha (and their brother Lazarus) crop up elsewhere in the Bible and that's where we find out the name of their village. So now you know!

Martha had kindly invited Jesus into their home. I'm sure it was a welcome pit stop for Jesus after being on the road – a nice chance to put His feet up, have some food and drink and then be on His way again. Martha busied herself to make Jesus feel at home. Meanwhile her sister Mary didn't so much as lift a finger. She parked herself at Jesus' feet and was all ears, hanging on Jesus' every word. Just to let you know, in those days and in that neck of the woods it wasn't the done thing for a woman to sit at a man's feet. This place was reserved for the disciples of teachers (like Jesus) and in their

Jewish religion (that's Judaism for those of you who don't know) it was almost unheard of for a woman to be a disciple.

That didn't seem to bother Martha. What had got under her skin was that while she was running herself ragged doing all the chores, Mary was doing diddly-squat (nothing).

Much to Martha's surprise Jesus didn't takes sides with her against her idle sister. On the contrary! Jammy Mary got the big thumbs-up from Him for what she was doing. Want to know why? Of course you do.

48
MALTA MARVELS

Some people are always getting into scrapes and a guy called Paul (who crops up in the New Testament bit of the Bible) was one such person. In the course of his travels to tell people about Jesus he got into one pickle after another. Be it getting thrown into prison, robbed, attacked, stoned, flogged or shipwrecked, Paul had the T-shirt (which is another way of saying that he'd done it all).

We catch up with the unfortunate fella shortly after one of those shipwrecks I just mentioned. This time he (along with 275 others) was washed up on the Mediterranean island of Malta. It was absolutely tipping it down so the islanders built the castaways a fire so they could dry off and keep warm. As if Paul hadn't had enough trouble for one day, a snake (driven out by the heat and smoke of the fire) sank its fangs into his hand. The long and short of it was that God protected the guy though and he didn't die.

The Maltese (no, they're not called Maltesers, however funny you might think it) were in two minds as to what to make of Paul. Was he a criminal and the snake bite was him getting his just deserts? But when he didn't die they changed their minds and thought that maybe he was a god instead?

While they were still having a good old ponder, Paul was about to put them straight.

The chief bod on Malta was a chap by the name of Publius. He lived nearby and invited Paul and co. to come and stay with him for a bit. How kind was that!

When Paul got wind that Publius' dad was really poorly he went to visit him. After praying to God Paul placed his hands on Publius' poorly pa and healed him in God's power.

Want to know what reaction this got on the island?

Look up Bible book Acts, chapter 28 and verses 9 and 10.

49
ALL IS REVEALED

Imagine worshipping something that you know nothing about. Crazy! That's what was going on in Athens many, many years ago. The star of our story (Paul) had done a runner from a place called Berea where he'd stirred up a near riot. All had been going well until a bunch of Jews who didn't like what Paul had to say about Jesus, showed up. Having said that, there were heaps of Jews who did like what Paul had to say about Jesus.

The Bereans (yep, that's what you call people from Berea) were keen to hear what Paul had to say about Jesus being God's Son who had come to this world to get us back to being friends with God. Loads of the Bereans became Christians, which really narked those jaded Jews. Fearing that Paul might get mauled by the mob his mates whisked him away to safety in Athens.

While Paul waited for his best buddies, Silas and Timothy, to join him, he did a spot of sight-seeing around the famous city. He was more than a little concerned to notice that the place was choc-a-bloc full of idols.

Paul set up shop in Athens and began to talk to anybody who would listen about Jesus. He tried to persuade them that the idols that they worshipped were nothing more than lumps of metal or stone. He spoke in the Jewish synagogues (which were like their churches) and he spoke in the marketplace.

The Atheneans had a bit of a reputation for discussing new ideas and what Paul had to say certainly got their attention. To be honest most of them thought he was talking a load of nonsense but they still wanted to hear more. So Paul got invited to speak at the Areopagus, a rocky hill where important business was done.

Paul told them that when he'd been looking round Athens he'd seen an altar with the inscription: 'TO AN UNKNOWN GOD'. Fortunately for the jammy Atheneans Paul knew precisely who this God was and he was now about to tell 'em.

HANDY HIDEAWAY

I n the Old Testament bit of the Bible there are loads and loads of laws and rules which God gave to His people, the Israelites. Although some of them might appear a bit strict (or even strange) they were all designed for the benefit of the Israelites. One thing that God took particularly seriously was the value of human life. God had made people as the icing on the cake of His creation and He was keen to ensure that no person was treated badly, not if He could help it.

So that human life didn't get taken lightly, God made laws for people to keep and He set punishments for breaking those laws. The bottom line is that if you murdered someone you were for the chop yourself. But the death penalty wasn't only reserved for murderers. Anyone caught attacking their parents would have to suffer the same fate.

And if you were considering kidnapping someone then best to think again. If you were caught red-handed holding someone hostage, or had sold them on for a quick buck, then it was curtains for you also.

In Bible book Joshua we read about how the Israelites were about to settle down in the land of Canaan which God had given them and which, after many battles, they'd finally conquered.

God told Joshua (their leader) to pick a handful of cities throughout the land which would be called cities of refuge. What was that all about? I'll tell you.

If you know anything about God you'll know that He is a fair God. This was jolly good news if you'd gone and *accidently* killed someone.

If you fell into this category your best bet was to hot-foot it to one of these cities of refuge pronto and claim asylum. Sounds jammy to me but to find out how you could get off scot-free here's what to do.

Check out Bible book Joshua, chapter 20 and read verses 4 to 6.

NATIONAL DISTRIBUTORS

UK: (and countries not listed below)
CWR, Waverley Abbey House, Waverley Lane, Farnham, Surrey GU9 8EP.
Tel: (01252) 784700 Outside UK (44) 1252 784700 Email: mail@cwr.org.uk

AUSTRALIA: KI Entertainment, Unit 21 317-321 Woodpark Road, Smithfield, New South Wales 2164. Tel: 1 800 850 777 Fax: 02 9604 3699
Email: sales@kientertainment.com.au

CANADA: David C Cook Distribution Canada, PO Box 98, 55 Woodslee Avenue, Paris, Ontario N3L 3E5. Tel: 1800 263 2664 Email: sandi.swanson@davidccook.ca

GHANA: Challenge Enterprises of Ghana, PO Box 5723, Accra.
Tel: (021) 222437/223249 Fax: (021) 226227 Email: ceg@africaonline.com.gh

HONG KONG: Cross Communications Ltd, 1/F, 562A Nathan Road, Kowloon.
Tel: 2780 1188 Fax: 2770 6229 Email: cross@crosshk.com

INDIA: Crystal Communications, 10-3-18/4/1, East Marredpalli, Secunderabad – 500026, Andhra Pradesh. Tel/Fax: (040) 27737145
Email: crystal_edwj@rediffmail.com

KENYA: Keswick Books and Gifts Ltd, PO Box 10242-00400, Nairobi.
Tel: (020) 2226047/312639 Email: sales.keswick@africaonline.co.ke

MALAYSIA: Canaanland, No. 25 Jalan PJU 1A/41B, NZX Commercial Centre, Ara Jaya, 47301 Petaling Jaya, Selangor. Tel: (03) 7885 0540/1/2 Fax: (03) 7885 0545
Email: info@canaanland.com.my

Salvation Publishing & Distribution Sdn Bhd, 23 Jalan SS 2/64, 47300 Petaling Jaya, Selangor. Tel: (03) 78766411/78766797 Fax: (03) 78757066/78756360
Email: info@salvationbookcentre.com

NEW ZEALAND: KI Entertainment, Unit 21 317-321 Woodpark Road, Smithfield, New South Wales 2164, Australia. Tel: 0 800 850 777 Fax: +612 9604 3699
Email: sales@kientertainment.com.au

NIGERIA: FBFM, Helen Baugh House, 96 St Finbarr's College Road, Akoka, Lagos.
Tel: (01) 7747429/4700218/825775/827264 Email: fbfm_1@yahoo.com

PHILIPPINES: OMF Literature Inc, 776 Boni Avenue, Mandaluyong City.
Tel: (02) 531 2183 Fax: (02) 531 1960 Email: gloadlaon@omflit.com

SINGAPORE: Alby Commercial Enterprises Pte Ltd, 95 Kallang Avenue #04-00, AIS Industrial Building, 339420. Tel: (65) 629 27238 Fax: (65) 629 27235
Email: marketing@alby.com.sg

SOUTH AFRICA: Struik Christian Books, Wembly Square, 1st Floor, Solan Street, Gardens, Cape Town, South Africa, 8001. Tel: (021) 460 5400 Fax: (021) 461 7662
Email: info@struikchristianmedia.co.za

SRI LANKA: Christombu Publications (Pvt) Ltd, Bartleet House, 65 Braybrooke Place, Colombo 2. Tel: (9411) 2421073/2447665 Email: dhanad@bartleet.com

USA: David C Cook Distribution Canada, PO Box 98, 55 Woodslee Avenue, Paris, Ontario N3L 3E5, Canada. Tel: 1800 263 2664 Email: sandi.swanson@davidccook.ca

CWR is a Registered Charity – Number 294387

CWR is a Limited Company registered in England – Registration Number 1990308

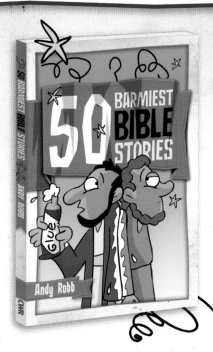

50 Barmiest Bible Stories

Loads of pretty barmy things happened back in Bible times! Andy Robb, author of the *Boring Bible* series, has collected together the barmiest passages of Scripture in *50 Barmiest Bible Stories*. Andy's witty and conversational style plus colourful illustrations, brings God's Word to life for children.

ISBN: 978-1-85345-852-1

50 Goriest Bible Stories
ISBN:
978-1-85345-530-8

50 Craziest Bible Stories
ISBN:
978-1-85345-490-5

50 Weirdest Bible Stories
ISBN:
978-1-85345-489-9

50 Wildest Bible Stories
ISBN:
978-1-85345-529-2

For current prices visit www.cwr.org.uk

MORE FROM ANDY ROBB

Professor Bumblebrain offers some exciting explanations, colourful cartoons and (ahem) 'hilarious' jokes answering these important questions:

Who is God? What is He like? Where does He live? How can I get to know Him?
ISBN: 978-1-85345-579-7

Who's the bravest? Who's the funniest? Who's the jammiest? Who's the strongest?
ISBN: 978-1-85345-578-0

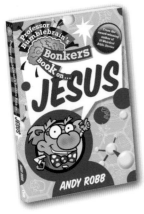

Who is Jesus? Where did He come from? What was His mission? What's it to me?
ISBN: 978-1-85345-623-7

Who made the universe? How old is planet earth? What about dinosaurs? Was there really a worldwide flood?
ISBN: 978-1-85345-622-0

Get into God's Word

Topz is a popular bimonthly devotional for 7- to 11-year-olds.

The Topz Gang teach children biblical truths through daily Bible readings, word games, puzzles, riddles, cartoons, competitions and simple prayers.

Only **£2.85** each
or **£15.50** (UK) for a year's subscription (six issues)

YP's is a dynamic bimonthly devotional for 11- to 15-year-olds.

Each issue is packed with cool graphics, special features and articles, plus daily Bible readings and notes for two months.

Only **£2.85** each
or **£15.50** (UK) for a year's subscription (six issues)

Prices correct at time of printing and exclusive of p&p

Learn about life with lots of LAUGHS
from Alexa Tewkesbury

Danny's Daring Days

Talented footballer Danny learns how to step out in faith, believing that God and His love will always be with him.

ISBN: 978-1-85345-502-5

John's Jam-Packed Jottings

John learns about loyalty to Jesus and God's forgiving nature.

ISBN: 978-1-85345-503-2

Josie's Jazzy Journal

Josie, with the help of best friend Sarah, learns how to show God's love.

ISBN: 978-1-85345-457-8

Paul's Potty Pages

Paul from the Topz Gang tries to impress the new American girl in his class, with disastrous results!

ISBN: 978-1-85345-456-1

Benny's Barmy Bits

Discover with Benny how God wants to be the most important part of our lives.

ISBN: 978-1-85345-431-8

Sarah's Secret Scribblings

Join Sarah from the Topz Gang as she learns to pray for people who upset her, discovers that everyone is special to God, and more.

ISBN: 978-1-85345-432-5

Dave's Dizzy Doodles

Dave discovers it's never too late for God to turn things around.

ISBN: 978-1-85345-552-0

Gruff & Saucy's Topzy-Turvy Tales

Gruff and Saucy learn that, although it's sometimes hard trying to live God's way, He gives us the Holy Spirit to help us.

ISBN: 978-1-85345-553-7

These special editions of *Topz Secret Diaries* will help you discover things about yourself and God with questions and quizzes, puzzles, word searches, doodles, lists to write and more.

Topz Secret Diaries: Boys Only

ISBN: 978-1-85345-596-4

Topz Secret Diaries: Just for Girls

ISBN: 978-1-85345-597-1

For current prices visit www.cwr.org.uk